P9-EEC-590

EDGE
BOOKS™

BRUTAL GAMES!

HISTORY'S MOST DANGEROUS SPORTS

by Marty Gitlin

CAPSTONE PRESS
a capstone imprint

Edge Books are published by Capstone Press,
1710 Roe Crest Drive, North Mankato, Minnesota 56003
www.capstonepub.com

Copyright © 2014 by Capstone Press, a Capstone imprint. All rights reserved.
No part of this publication may be reproduced in whole or in part, or stored
in a retrieval system, or transmitted in any form or by any means, electronic,
mechanical, photocopying, recording, or otherwise, without written
permission of the publisher.

Library of Congress Cataloging-in-Publication Data
Gitlin, Marty.
Brutal Games!: History's Most Dangerous Sports / by Marty Gitlin.
pages cm—(Edge books. Dangerous history)
Includes bibliographical references and index.
Summary: "Gives detailed information on some of history's most
dangerous sports"—Provided by publisher.
ISBN 978-1-4765-0125-3 (library binding)
ISBN 978-1-4765-3381-0 (eBook PDF)
1. Extreme sports—Juvenile literature. 2. Endurance sports—Juvenile
literature. I. Title.
GV749.7.G58 2014
796.04'6—dc23   2013018224

Editorial Credits
Jeni Wittrock, editor; Sarah Bennett, designer; Marcie Spence,
media researcher; Jennifer Walker, production specialist

Photo Credits
Bridgeman Art Library: Phoenix Art Museum, Arizona, 27; Corbis: Henry
Watkins & Yibran Aragon/Reuters, 25, HO/Reuters, 20; Getty Images:
Josh Hedges/Zuffa LLC, 17, 19, Universal History Archive, 1; Shutterstock:
Christopher Halloran, 9, Clive Watkins, cover (bottom right), Evgeniya Moroz,
cover (bottom left), imagemaker, 5, Joanne Weston, cover (top right), justasc,
11, Margo Harrison, cover (top left), My Good Images, 23, Neale Cousland,
15, Rich Carey, 28–29, Robert H. Creigh, 13, Scott Kapich, 21, Vitalii
Nesterchuk, 7

Printed in the United States of America in Stevens Point, Wisconsin.
032013   007227WZF13

TABLE OF CONTENTS

HISTORY'S DAREDEVILS

Imagine jumping off a skyscraper, riding a bucking bull, or charging at an opponent on horseback. Sound appealing? The boldest of athletes think so! Throughout history, athletes have risked their lives for sport. Some of them chose to compete, while others had no choice. Some performed with no one watching, while others amazed huge crowds.

Fighting wild animals or leaping off tall buildings is not for the faint of heart. Many people have paid the ultimate price for their sports. Some people consider these risk-taking athletes to be foolish. Others admire them. Either way, the daredevils who have taken part in history's most dangerous sports have an incredible sense of adventure.

A BASE jumper takes the plunge.

BASE JUMPING

BASE jumpers leap from buildings and bound off bridges. They jump off canyon ledges and antenna towers.

In 1913 Slovak inventor Stefan Banic was the first person to successfully BASE jump. He leaped off the 41st floor of a building in Washington, D.C. Banic survived the jump using a parachute that he invented. The following year he made the first successful parachute jump from an airplane. Banic's parachute design played an important role in **aviation** safety for many years.

Because of the risks involved with BASE jumping, it is illegal in many places. Jumpers have barely enough time to open a parachute. If a jumper hesitates or the chute malfunctions, there's no time for a backup plan. But hitting the ground isn't what causes most injuries. Slamming into the object they are jumping from is what kills many BASE jumpers.

Researchers at the University of Stavanger in Norway studied 20,850 jumps off the Kjerag massif cliffs from 1995 to 2005. According to the study results, one in every 2,317 jumps resulted in death. One in 254 jumps resulted in injuries such as broken bones or **concussions**.

aviation—the science of building and flying aircraft

concussion—an injury to the brain caused by a hard blow to the head

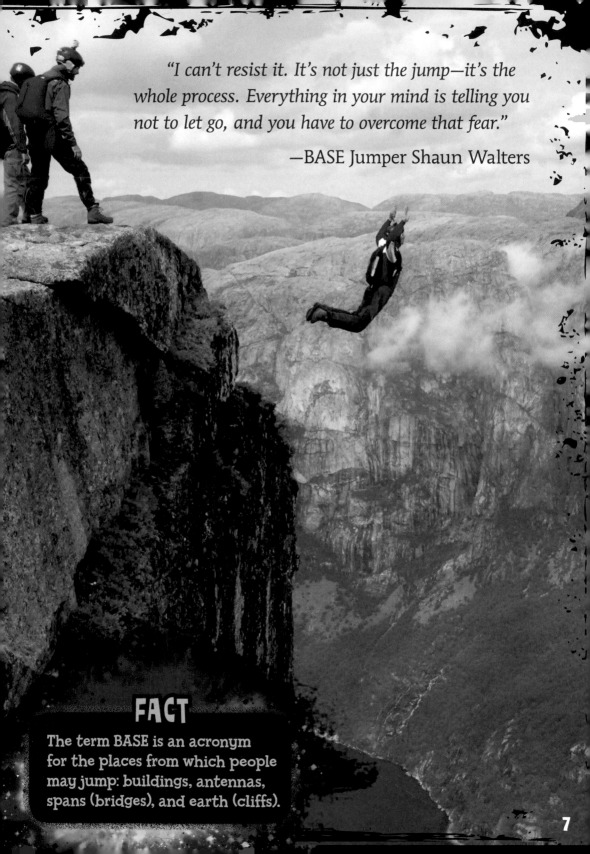

"I can't resist it. It's not just the jump—it's the whole process. Everything in your mind is telling you not to let go, and you have to overcome that fear."

—BASE Jumper Shaun Walters

FACT

The term BASE is an acronym for the places from which people may jump: buildings, antennas, spans (bridges), and earth (cliffs).

The idea behind bull riding is simple. A rider tries to stay on a bucking bull for eight seconds. But a lot can happen in that short time. A rider may be thrown off, stomped, and **gored** by a 1,500-pound (680-kilogram) beast. Other times the event is over before it officially begins. Riders struggle to stay onboard even as the bull exits the **chute**.

Bulls buck with unbelievable force. For the fans, it makes for an incredible show. Riders take extra steps to encourage the bull to buck, not run, during his outing. Riders' dulled spurs, a dangling bell, and a tight **flank strap** give bulls all the more reason to buck their hardest. With just one hand, riders grip a rope secured to the thrashing animals. As the bull beneath revolts, a rider uses all his skills and strength to keep from crashing to the ground.

gore—to pierce with a horn

chute—a narrow pathway leading to the rodeo arena

flank strap—a strap tied around a bull's sensitive flanks to encourage it to buck rather than run

FLANK STRAP

SPURS

BELL

"It is dangerous, and you can die doing it. But the way I look at it, shoot, you can get hurt doing about anything—walking down the steps, driving down the road. Yeah, it's more apt to happen in what we do, but I was raised to rodeo."

— professional bull rider J.B. Mauney

A rider who is bucked off must flee the angry animal's head, horns, and hooves. A thrown rider scrambles to safety while four **bullfighters** distract the bull. Even with bullfighters' help, 70 percent of bull-riding fatalities are a result of being struck by these powerful animals.

One might think the eight-second rule was made to protect riders from the dangers of the sport. But the rule is actually meant to prevent the bulls from becoming exhausted or injured. A limited bucking time helps top bulls stay spirited and strong for future competitions. Riders can only hope for the same outcome.

Bullfighters rush in to help a thrown rider.

FACT

Some bull riders believe they can't balance as well while wearing a helmet. But riders who don't wear one are far more likely to be badly injured or killed. A 1989-2009 University of Calgary study showed that none of the riders killed by a head injury was wearing a helmet.

bullfighter—one of four aids who distract a rodeo bull that has thrown its rider; bullfighters allow riders to escape to safety

LIVING DANGEROUSLY

Since 2007 researchers at the University of Calgary in Canada have studied severe sports injuries. The researchers determined that bull riding is the riskiest organized sport in the world. One study reported 49 bull-riding accidents that caused "life-changing" injuries from 1989 to 2009. Nearly half of the accidents resulted in death. The other injuries were serious, long-term disabilities such as damage to internal organs or the loss of limbs.

JOUSTING

Imagine living in England in the 1300s. King Edward III has gathered his finest jousters. They are set to battle the best jousters from France. The teams line up, shoulder to shoulder, astride their finest horses. Their metal armor gleams in the sun. The lines of jousters face each other, ready to attack. Each fighter holds a long, sharpened wooden **lance** pointed at his rival in the opposite line. Horses stomp and snort, eager for battle. Then the two sides charge forward.

Jousting has historically been known as "the sport of kings." It began as a way for a knight to sharpen his fighting skills. A knight tried to injure his opponent or knock the opponent off his horse. Sometimes knights fought one-on-one. Other times groups of knights fought mock battles.

The first recorded jousting tournaments were held in 1066. These battles were not fought to the death, but they could easily become deadly.

Renaissance-themed events in Europe and North America host today's jousting matches. Unlike competitions of the past, the outcomes of these battles are usually planned. Jousters are skilled riders and actors who safely compete for audiences. Even the lances are made to shatter rather than pierce the opponent's armor.

Jousters charge full speed toward their opponents.

In 2011 the National Geographic TV channel aired a reality show called *Knights of Mayhem*. The show followed the lives of American **full-contact** professional jousters. These athletes are different from most jousters today. They fight to win without holding back. It is more like a real battle and less like an act for entertainment. Jousting champion Charlie Andrews was one jouster featured on the show. Andrews knows the risks of his sport, but his love of full-contact jousting keeps him competing. "You're gonna get hurt," he said. "The only question is when and how bad." Andrews' injuries have included a snapped collarbone, punctured lung, dislocated hip, and fractured back.

lance—a long spear

full contact—colliding on purpose and at full force

13

AUSTRALIAN RULES FOOTBALL

American football is dangerous. But at least the players wear protective gear. Those who play Australian rules football wear nothing but their uniforms. They collide at full speed as they fight for the ball. The average player suffers many serious injuries during his or her career. The most common injuries are to the ankles, knees, and shoulders.

Australian rules football is known as "footy." Two teams of 18 players compete on an oval field. To earn points, players try to kick the ball through posts guarded by the other team. Players smash into each other to control the ball and score points. The hardest hits send players airborne before they crash to the ground.

FOOTY IN AMERICA

In 1996 footy made its way to the United States. The first teams were based in Cincinnati, Ohio and Louisville, Kentucky. Soon more teams formed. In 1997 the United States Australian Football League (USAFL) was born. The USAFL now includes dozens of teams and a women's division. The USAFL holds a yearly tournament to crown a champion team for the men's and women's divisions.

Hard-hitting footy games are never short on action.

ULTIMATE FIGHTING CHAMPIONSHIP (UFC)

Ultimate Fighting Championship (UFC) fighters face off in a steel cage. They kick and punch their opponents and slam them to the floor. They throw them into the chain-link cage and twist them into painful positions.

To gain publicity, the earliest UFC fights were advertised as having no rules. The lack of weight classes sometimes resulted in 400-pound (181-kg) fighters battling opponents half their size. These bloody fights allowed hair pulling, choking, and elbowing fighters in the face. It was unlike anything U.S. crowds had ever seen.

UFC fighting debuted in the United States in 1993. It was largely based on a Brazilian fight style called Vale Tudo, which means "anything goes." Many U.S. officials believed the earliest UFC fights were too violent, and many states banned UFC matches. By the year 2000, UFC had added a set of rules to increase safety and fairness. Soon states began to accept the new, safer UFC terms, and many bans lifted. Today men and women compete in UFC matches throughout the United States and around the world.

Mike Swick pins Damarques Johnson against the cage in a 2012 fight.

FACT

UFC fighters are masters of mixed **martial arts** (MMA). They train also in boxing, kickboxing, sumo, and wrestling.

martial arts—styles of self-defense and fighting, such as tae kwon do, judo, and karate

17

UFC matches are so intense that they are kept short. Championship matches are five rounds of five minutes each. Other matches are three rounds of five minutes each. The fighters get one minute to rest between each round.

UFC fighting isn't just one of the most dangerous sports in the United States. It is also one of the most popular. More than 9 million fans watched UFC matches on **pay-per-view** TV in 2010.

A FIGHTING HYBRID

Which sport has better fighters: karate or wrestling? Ultimate fighting first gained its appeal by matching fighters from different sports. Boxers faced off against sumo wrestlers. Kickboxers went toe-to-toe against jiu-jitsu champions. Excited fans gathered to watch these unusual fights and determine the ultimate combat sport.

To beat such a wide range of opponents, UFC fighters began training in multiple styles of fighting. Soon UFC fighters were known for being skilled in many martial arts and combat sports. The result was a brand new sport with hybrid athletes trained in many different fields.

pay-per-view—a service for cable TV viewers in which customers view a single movie or televised event for a fee

Frank Edgar delivers a hit to Sean Sherk in a 2009 match.

"It's about having confidence in yourself. I'm not afraid of that man across from me."

—UFC light heavyweight fighter Ken Shamrock

HIGH-ALTITUDE CLIMBING

In 1953 a daring mountain-climbing **expedition** set out. The team had their sights set on reaching the top of Mount Everest in Nepal. The dizzying peak rises more than 29,000 feet (8,839 meters) into the Asian sky. The previous seven expeditions had failed—one claiming the life of famous climber George Leigh-Mallory.

In May 1953 most of the 11 team members had turned back from exhaustion. Only Sir Edmund Hillary and his guide Tenzing Norgay continued. These brave adventurers became the first people to scale the peak of the highest mountain in the world. They became heroes to millions.

FACT

The temperature atop Mount Kilimanjaro in Tanzania, Africa can fall to minus 15 degrees Fahrenheit (-26 degrees Celsius).

Edmund Hillary and Tenzing Norgay

expedition—a group of people on a journey with a goal, such as climbing a mountain

Mount McKinley, Alaska

WHERE TO CLIMB

In 2008 National Geographic magazine created a list of the top 10 best mountains to climb in the world. The only American peak ranked in the top 10 was Mount McKinley in Alaska. It rises nearly 18,000 feet (5,486 m) from its base. The magazine praised the mountain's beautiful views. The top honors went to Mount Khuiten in Mongolia. The mountain rests along the borders of Russia and China. The breathtaking landscape and the kindness of the local people are just a few reasons Khuiten topped the list.

Today many daredevils follow in Hillary's and Norgay's footsteps. These high-altitude climbers face many dangers.

The most obvious is the risk of falling to the rocks below. But a more common threat is the cold. The higher the climb, the colder temperatures become. Skin freezes at 32 degrees Fahrenheit (0 degrees Celsius). Frostbite and restricted blood flow result.

High-altitude climbers also often suffer from the lack of oxygen at high altitudes, which makes breathing difficult. The body responds to having less oxygen by sending more blood to the brain. The extra blood can leak into the brain and cause it to swell. Brain swelling causes brain damage and sometimes death.

FACT

Avalanches can be a major threat to mountain climbers. In 1990, 40 out of 140 climbers scaling Lenin Peak in the Soviet Union were killed by one avalanche. It is considered one of the worst tragedies in climbing history.

avalanche—a mass of snow, rocks, ice, or soil that slides down a mountain slope

MOUNT EVEREST DEATHS ABOVE BASE CAMP 1921-2006	
objective hazards (icefall collapses, crevasses, and falling rock)	67
falls	46
high altitude illness	17
hypothermia	11
sudden death	7
unclassified	17
disappeared	27

An avalanche can travel 200 miles (322 km) per hour or faster.

"Life is brought down to the basics: if you are warm ...
healthy, not thirsty or hungry, then you are not on a mountain."

—high-altitude climber Chris Darwin

CAVE DIVING

Cave divers uncover mysteries underwater and underground. Divers travel through winding networks of tunnels that are almost completely underwater. The thrill of seeing places few humans have ever seen excites some divers. Others dive to search for artifacts hidden for hundreds of years. Still others seek the bones of divers who did not make it out alive.

Cave diving comes with great risk. An average of 20 cave divers are killed every year. Since 1950, 400 cave divers have died in the caves and caverns of Florida alone. A tunnel's collapse can easily result in a diver's death. But even in stable tunnels, there are many dangers. In the dark, winding passageways, inexperienced divers lose their sense of direction. Getting lost might mean the divers run out of air before they can get out of the caves. For cave divers, getting proper training and staying calm under stress are essential.

FACT

Another name for cave diving is "underwater speleology." The U.S. National Speleological Society offers a membership just for cave divers. They define a successful dive as "one you return from."

Cave divers explore in Cenote Dos Ojos, Mexico.

GLADIATOR GAMES

The gladiator games may have claimed more lives than any other sport in history. Before a roaring crowd, these brave fighters battled each other and wild animals in ancient Rome.

Historians have limited knowledge about the brutal sport. They do know that gladiators fought between about 264 BC and AD 440. Prisoners of war or suspected criminals were believed to be recruited to fight. A few gladiators were former soldiers or wealthy Romans seeking fame and fortune. Although not every match resulted in death, most gladiators were killed before they reached age 30.

One man wins one fight, is slaughtered immediately after in the next. The winner is sent against another man to be killed. It is a round robin of death ... Death is the fighter's only exit.

—historian Seneca, speaking about the gladiator games, AD 40

FACT

Gladiator battles in large arenas were not the first gladiator games. Before they were public events, the games were often held during funeral services for important Romans.

TIMELINE OF DANGEROUS SPORTS

264 BC
The funeral of Junius Brutus includes the first recorded gladiator games.

AD 1066
Frenchman Godfrey de Preuilly mentions a jousting tournament for the first time on record.

1858
The first Australian rules football matches are held.

1993
The first Ultimate Fighting Championship (UFC) event is held in Denver, Colorado.

1953
Sir Edmund Hillary and Tenzing Norgay become the first people to scale Mount Everest.

1913
Slovak inventor Stefan Banic takes the first successful BASE jump. A parachute he designs ensures his survival after he leaps off a 41-story building in Washington, D.C.

1872
The first organized rodeo is held in Cheyenne, Wyoming.

1941
The National Speleological Society is formed.

GLOSSARY

avalanche (A-vuh-lanch)—a mass of snow, rocks, ice, or soil that slides down a mountain slope

aviation (ay-vee-AY-shuhn)—the science of building and flying aircraft

bullfighter (BULL-fyter)—one of four aids who distract a rodeo bull that has thrown its rider; bullfighters allow riders to escape to safety

chute (SHOOT)—a narrow pathway that leads bulls and riders to the rodeo arena

concussion (kuhn-KUH-shuhn)—an injury to the brain caused by a hard blow to the head

expedition (ek-spuh-DI-shuhn)—a group of people on a journey with a goal, such as climbing to a mountain top

flank strap (FLANK STRAP)—a strap tied around a bull's sensitive flanks to encourage it to buck rather than run

full contact (FULL KON-takt)—colliding on purpose and at full force

gore (GORE)—to pierce with a horn

lance (LANSS)—a long spear

martial arts (MAR-shuhl ARTS)—styles of self-defense and fighting, such as tae kwon do, judo, and karate

pay-per-view (PAY-PUR-VYOO)—a service for cable TV viewers in which customers order and view a single movie or televised event for a fee

READ MORE

Burgan, Michael. *Life as a Gladiator: An Interactive History Adventure.* Warriors. Mankato, Minn.: Capstone Press, 2011.

Goldsworthy, Steve. *A Daredevil's Guide to Stunts.* Daredevils' Guides. North Mankato, Minn.: Capstone Press, 2013.

Hamilton, John. *Inside the Octagon.* Xtreme UFC. Edina, Minn.: ABDO Pub. Co., 2011.

INTERNET SITES

FactHound offers a safe, fun way to find Internet sites related to this book. All of the sites on FactHound have been researched by our staff.

Here's all you do:

Visit *www.facthound.com*

Type in this code: 9781476501253

 Check out projects, games and lots more at **www.capstonekids.com**

INDEX